Contents

Basic equipment	4
Hints and tips	6
Snake ring	8
Water droplets	10
Spring flowers	14
Delightfully chic	16
Tahitian treasures	18
Boiled sweets	22
Roses	24
Marbles	26
He loves me, he loves me not	30
Petal ring	32
Morning dew	34
Total diva	36
Pyramid	40
Ribbon of beads	42
Sleeping Beauty	44
Indian summer	48
On the banks of the Nile	50
Futuristic	52
Ring of romance	54
Holiday hairclips	56
Queen of the Night	58
Snow flowers	61
Suppliers	64

 Very easy Easy  Tricky

Basic equipment

Beads

All the beads used in this book are glass beads, which are inexpensive to buy. You can find them in craft stores, specialist shops and department store haberdasheries. You could make your jewellery using plastic beads, but bear in mind that the finished products will have less sparkle.

Seed beads

Seed beads 1–3mm ($1/16$–$1/8$in) are the smallest beads you can buy. They come in many colours and you can find them in matte, metallic, clear, mother-of-pearl and glitter finishes. There are three types: round seed beads, bugles (long) and micro bugles (small rectangles).

Faceted beads

Faceted beads are slightly oval in shape and are made from Bohemian crystal glass (named after the place where they are made). To make the designs in this book you will need 3mm ($1/8$in), 4mm ($5/32$in) and 6mm ($3/8$in) beads. Faceted beads come in over 60 colours, some with an iridescent finish.

Drop beads

Drop beads look like droplets of water. They are flame-worked and have a smooth surface. Drop beads are quite new and come in over 60 colours, in matte, iridescent and glitter finishes and 4mm ($5/32$in) and 6mm ($3/8$in) sizes.

Cat's eye beads

These beads, inspired by natural agate, have great colouring. Round or faceted, they come in 16 colours in 3–8mm ($1/8$–$5/16$in) sizes.

Mother-of-pearl beads

These smooth, round beads, 4mm ($5/32$in), 6mm ($3/8$in) and 8mm ($5/16$in), are wonderful imitations of cultured pearls. Made from glass, they are soaked several times in a fish scale solution, to which a little silver is added before the final colour is applied.

Miracle beads

Miracle beads, 4mm ($5/32$in), 6mm ($3/8$in) and 8mm ($5/16$in), are round and appear to contain a bead within a bead. The beads have a lucite core with a silver mirror plate finish and are coated in several layers of coloured lacquer. Beware of plastic imitations!

... and many more

Cord and wire

Nylon cord

This clear, flexible cord is used to make up most of the jewellery designs in this book. The nylon cord used in this book is 0.25mm (¹/₁₀₀in) in diameter.

Copper wire

Use this 0.18mm (32 gauge) diameter wire to add shape to your designs. It comes in seven colours to match your beads.

Tools

All-purpose pliers

These pliers can cut, crush and flatten and have rounded tips for shaping copper wire and closing jump rings on bracelets, necklaces and pendants. You can also use them to cut nylon cord.

Beading needle

A beading needle is useful for threading beads on to sewing thread and other very flexible materials.

Jewellery glue

Use this glue to secure bead tips on bracelets and necklaces and for gluing your work on to hairslides, Alice bands and hairclips.

Findings

You will need findings to make bracelets, pendants, necklaces and earrings. They come in gold, silver and copper versions. Use nickel-free findings to prevent skin irritation.

Bead tips

These clam shell beads conceal knots on bracelets and necklaces. Buy bead tips with two shells that close vertically with a small hole for the threads in the centre. The larger versions will accommodate more threads.

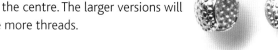

Clasps

Clasps come in a variety of types: barrel clasps, bolt rings, trigger clasps, and many more.

Small and large jump rings

Jump rings are secured on to bead tips or leather crimps to attach to the clasp.

Leather crimps

Leather crimps are used on ribbon and satin cord for hanging pendants.

Earrings

For pierced ears use studs or fishhook earwires. For non-pierced ears choose clip-on mounts.

Ribbons

You can hang your pendants from a number of different materials such as muslin or satin ribbons in a variety of widths. You can also use leather or cotton thonging.

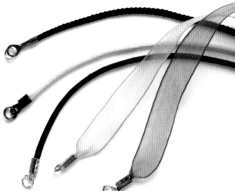

Hints and tips

Tip: before long you will start to amass lots of beads and accessories. Try to get hold of a container with a lid and small compartments so that you can keep similar colours and shapes together.

Preparation

Choose a design and lay out the beads required on an upside-down mouse mat to keep them from rolling off. Read through all the instructions and diagrams carefully so you understand how the design will work.

Divide your beads into small piles, one for each step. If a bead is missing or you have one too many beads at the end of a step then you will know there is a problem. Work slowly and check your work after every step to make sure you have made no mistakes.

Understanding the diagrams

The starting point is indicated by a red triangle. Different ends of cord and wire are shown in grey and black. Arrows at each end indicate the direction of the thread. In the first diagram all the beads will be in colour because they are added in the first step. In the second diagram, beads added in the previous step are shown paler. The coloured beads are the ones you add in that step. Lay out your beadwork the same way around as in the diagrams so you can follow them more easily. And don't forget that the text is there to help you as well.

Key principle

The jewellery in this book is made by crossing wires or cord through beads. To do this, thread on a bead and hold it in your fingers with 2cm (³/₄in) excess thread on one side. Thread the other cord through the bead in the opposite direction. This will give you one end coming out of each side, as shown in the diagram. Next, even up the ends so they are the same length. Keep them nice and tight in every step.

Rings
Making a ring base

Once you have finished making the top of a ring you should make up the ring base, the part that goes around your finger. Thread one or two seed beads on to each end of wire or cord, then cross them in another bead. Continue to work this way until your ring is the right size. When you have finished, add one or two seed beads to each end, just as you did at the start. Cross the ends in the bead opposite the starter bead to make your ring straight. Go back through all the beads in the ring in the opposite direction to strengthen the design. Cross the ends in your starter bead again and thread one end through the beads at the end of your ring: the two ends are now together. Now all you have to do is add the finishing touches.

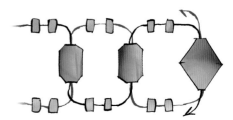

Finishing off a ring

Now that the ends are together, tie a very tight knot, then tie a surgeon's knot. It's simple! A surgeon's knot is similar to a normal knot, except for the fact that you wind one end around the other twice (as opposed to once in a normal knot). When you tighten a knot, hold the ends of the wire or cord as close to the beads as you can so as not to break them.

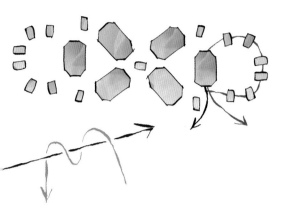

Finishing touches

Thread the two ends into the nearest bead. Pull them gently so the knots go into the bead. This has two benefits: the knots will be hidden and they won't move around. Lastly, thread each end into the next beads for at least 2cm ($^3/_4$in), then trim the excess with the pliers.

Bracelets and necklaces

Adding a bead tip

When working out the length of a bracelet or necklace, always take into account the length of the clasp, which will comprise bead tips at each end, a large jump ring at one end (for the clasp to hook on to) and a clasp at the other end.

To add the first bead tip, thread a seed bead into the centre of your cord or wire, then thread the two ends into the hole in the centre of the bead tip. Your seed bead should sit between the two clam shells of the bead tip. Add a little jewellery glue inside the bead tip, then close it with your pliers to secure.

Place a jump ring inside the hook in the bead tip and close the hook by holding it with the pliers around the jump ring and twisting the pliers gently. Repeat this process to attach the clasp to the hook in the bead tip at the other end. Next, attach the clasp to the ring. With the clasp and

rings attached to the start end of your item of jewellery you can alter the length of your cord easily if needed. Once you have finished work on your beads, thread the two ends into the second bead tip from the back. Thread a seed bead on to one of the ends, tie your two knots and secure in the same way as the first bead tip. Trim any excess. Your piece of jewellery is finished!

Finishing off a pendant

To finish off a pendant you will need two leather crimps, one large jump ring, one small jump ring and a clasp. If your ribbon is narrow, tie a knot in each end. Place the knot in one of the leather crimps. Use pliers to close one side of the crimp on to the ribbon and hold to keep it flat. Next, close the other side of the crimp on to the first and hold with your pliers to secure.

Open the large jump ring by separating the two ends with your pliers. To keep the ring in shape, pull one end towards you and the other in the opposite direction. Thread the ring into the loop in the leather crimp and close the ring by bringing the two ends together with your pliers. Open the small jump ring in the same way, thread it through the clasp and into the loop in the second leather crimp, and close. Attach your clasp to the large jump ring. Now your clasp is attached to one end of your ribbon. Thread your pendant on to the ribbon and check that the ribbon is the right length in a mirror. Finally, attach the second leather crimp to the ribbon in the same way as the first.

> **Tip:** if you intend keeping your ring for a long time, make it for your middle finger. If it gets too small you can then wear it on another, smaller finger.

> **Tip:** to keep your beads looking shiny, remove your jewellery when washing your hands. Water (hard water in particular) can damage beads.

Snake ring

Go back to the jungle with this simple snake-like ring.

1. Thread a faceted bead into the centre of the cord, add a seed bead to each side and cross the ends in another faceted bead. Continue to work in this way until your ring is the correct size, then add two more faceted beads.

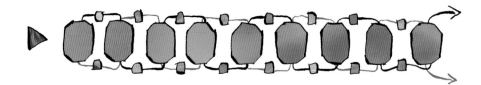

2. Place the two ends of your ring side by side, with two faceted beads overlapping at the top. Thread the upper cord into the seed bead in the centre, add a seed bead to the lower cord and cross the ends in a faceted bead. Repeat, then thread a seed bead on to each end of cord and cross them in a faceted bead.

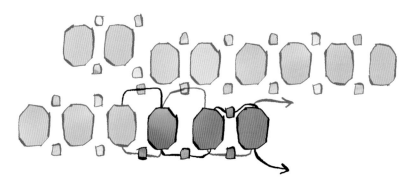

◄ Tip: use 4mm ($^5/_{32}$in) faceted beads for a chunkier looking ring.

3. Thread the ends of cord back through the seed beads and faceted beads so they meet, as shown in the diagram. Tie a knot and finish off (see page 6).

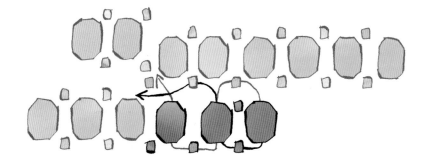

Water droplets

Be the belle of the ball with these eye-catching pieces!

Bracelet

1. Attach a bead tip as shown on page 7. Thread four red seed beads on to each end of the cord, then cross the ends in a bugle. Thread three red seed beads on to each end and cross them in an orange cat's eye bead, add another three red seed beads on to each end, then cross them in a bugle. Thread the second length of cord through the last bugle.

3. Working on the two cords together, thread on three yellow seed beads each side of the bugle bead. Cross the four ends in a cat's eye bead, add another three seed beads to each side, then cross them again in a bugle.

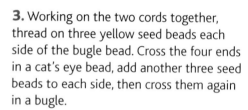

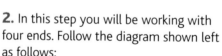

2. In this step you will be working with four ends. Follow the diagram shown left as follows:
- thread red and yellow drop beads and red seed beads on to one end each side;
- thread three yellow seed beads on to the other two ends, cross them in a cat's eye bead and add another three seed beads. Cross the four ends in a bugle bead.

4. Repeat steps 2 and 3 four times and then repeat step 2 once more. Repeat the motif in step 1 again, working in the opposite direction this time. To finish, attach a second bead tip and secure a jump ring to one end and a clasp to the other end (see page 7).

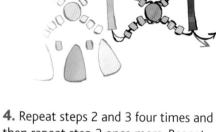

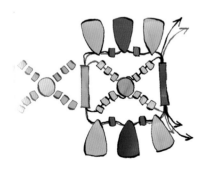

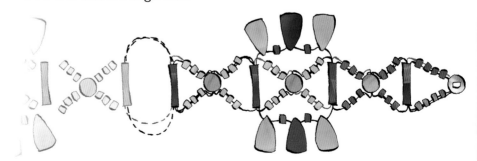

Pendant

1. Thread a yellow seed bead into the centre of the nylon cord. Add a bugle bead to the left end and drop beads and seed beads to the right end as shown in the diagram, then cross the two ends through a yellow seed bead.

2. Thread a bugle on to the left inner cord and drops and seed beads on to the right outer cord. Cross the ends through a yellow seed bead. Make up five similar motifs in this way. To close the circle of the pendant, add drops and seed beads to the outer cord, go through the starter seed bead, then cross the two ends through a bugle.

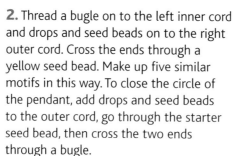

To make this pendant…

… you will need:

- 2 x 4mm (⁵/₃₂in) faceted cat's eye beads in orange
- 19 x 4mm (⁵/₃₂in) drop beads in yellow
- 12 x 4mm (⁵/₃₂in) drop beads in red
- 8 bugle beads in red
- seed beads in yellow and red
- 40cm (16in) red muslin ribbon 1cm (³/₈in) wide
- 2 leather crimps and 1 clasp
- 1 large and 1 small jump ring
- 50cm (20in) nylon cord
- all-purpose pliers

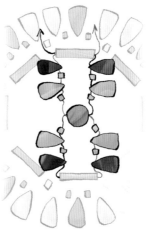

3. Add red and yellow drop beads and yellow seed beads on to each end of the cord and cross them in a cat's eye bead. Thread the drop beads and seed beads on to each end again and cross them in the bugle on the opposite side.

4. Thread each end through the yellow drop beads above the bugle. Thread five seed beads on to each end and cross them in a cat's eye bead. Add another five seed beads on to each end. Thread one of the ends of cord through a few beads to reach the other end. Tie the two ends together and finish off (see page 7).

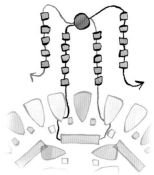

5. Thread a ribbon through the top loop and attach leather crimps and a clasp (see page 7).

Ring

1. Thread a red seed bead into the centre of the cord, then thread on a bugle either side and cross the ends through another bugle. Thread red and yellow drop beads on to each end of the cord, adding a red seed bead between each drop, then cross the ends in a bugle.

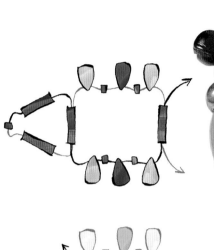

2. Thread three yellow seed beads on to each end of the cord. Cross the ends in a cat's eye bead and add another three seed beads to each end. Cross the ends in the left-hand bugle.

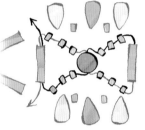

3. Thread three drop beads on to the lower cord, adding a red seed bead between each drop bead. Thread the cord back through the bugle. Thread the ends into the drop beads and seed beads (at the top and bottom), then cross them in the right-hand bugle. Repeat this process to add the drop beads on the right.

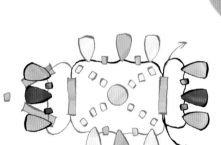
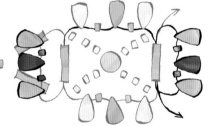
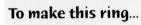

4. Thread a bugle bead on to each end of the cord, cross the ends in a red seed bead and then start work on the ring base (see page 6). Use the instructions given on page 6 to finish off your ring.

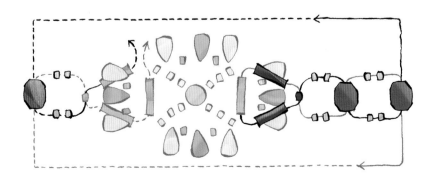

To make this ring…

… you will need:
- 1 x 4mm (^{5}/$_{32}$in) faceted cat's eye bead in orange
- 8 x 4mm (^{5}/$_{32}$in) drop beads in yellow
- 4 x 4mm (^{5}/$_{32}$in) drop beads in red
- 6 bugle beads in red
- 4mm (^{5}/$_{32}$in) red faceted beads and red and yellow seed beads for the ring base
- 50cm (20in) nylon cord
- all-purpose pliers

Spring flowers

Transform pretty, flower-shaped buttons into beads. This trendy necklace is guaranteed to be a great success.

1. Thread two peach seed beads into the centre of the cord, then thread the two ends of the cord into the holes of a mauve button and a peach button. Thread 11 peach seed beads on to the right end. Position a mauve button on top of a peach button and thread the cord through one of the holes in the buttons. Add two peach seed beads, then thread the cord back through the other hole so it comes out underneath the buttons. Repeat this process twice to the right. The seed beads will be hidden behind the buttons.

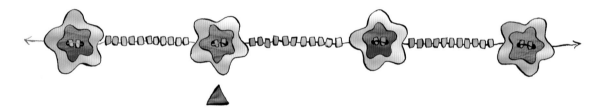

2. Continue working in this way, this time using only one button at a time, to add three peach buttons to each side.

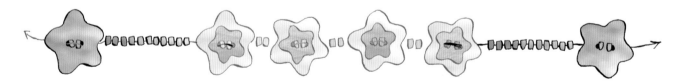

3. Now add a second layer of buttons. Take the other length of cord and thread the two ends into the holes of a mauve button from the back. Cross them in two peach seed beads. Thread four mauve seed beads on to each end and thread them from either side through the two peach seed beads you added in step 1. Add four mauve seed beads and two peach seed beads to the left-hand cord. Thread the cord from the front into the second hole in a mauve button and bring it out at the front through the other hole. Go back through the two peach seed beads, add four mauve seed beads and go into the next two peach seed beads. Repeat three times on the left and four times on the right.

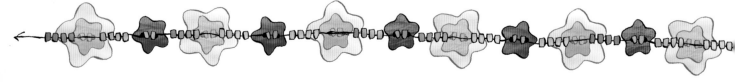

4. When you have added four mauve seed beads on top of the last button to the right, thread the two cords together into a faceted bead, then thread four peach seed beads on to each end. Repeat this process seven times to the right and eight times to the left. Finish with a mauve faceted bead at each end. Add bead tips to both ends, then attach a jump ring to one end and a clasp to the other (see page 7).

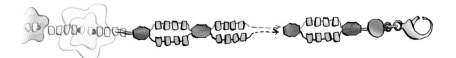

Delightfully chic

To make this bracelet…

… you will need:

- 36 bugle beads in silver
- seed beads in violet
- 2 bead tips
- jewellery glue
- 1 clasp
- 1 jump ring
- 1m (40in) nylon cord
- all-purpose pliers

Makes a 13cm (5in) bracelet (minus clasp).

This chic and trendy bracelet is very easy to make. Your friends will be so impressed that they will all want one!

1. Attach a jump ring and the first of the bead tips to a seed beed at the centre of the cord (see page 7). Thread four seed beads on to each end of cord and cross them in a bugle bead.

2. Thread five seed beads on to the lower cord and thread the end back through the second seed bead. Add a seed bead, then cross the two ends in a bugle bead. Repeat this motif using the upper cord. Continue to work in this way, adding seed beads at the top and then the bottom, until your bracelet is the right size.

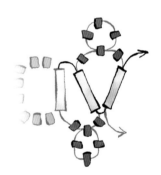

3. To finish off, thread five seed beads on to the lower cord and thread the cord back through the second bead. Thread on one more seed bead. Cross your ends in a bugle bead. Thread four seed beads on to each end and attach a second bead tip. Add a ring and clasp (see page 7).

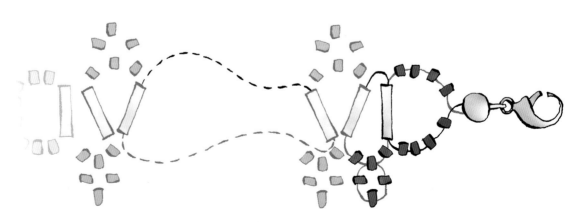

Tahitian treasures

Capture sun, sea and sand in this floral bracelet and ring in Tahitian colours. To complete the look, add a matching hair band.

Adding a flower

Ring

1. Thread on three bicone beads and a seed bead and cross the ends in a fourth bicone. Thread a seed bead on to the inner cord and two bicones on to the outer cord and cross them in another bicone. Repeat twice. Thread two bicones on to the outer cord, thread the cord into the starter bicone and cross the ends in a seed bead.

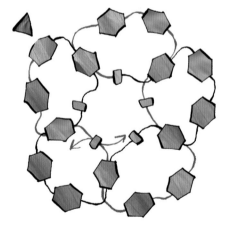

2. Thread a flower-shaped bead on to the two ends from underneath, then add a seed bead. Thread the two ends back through the hole in the flower and come back out on the underside. The seed bead will secure the flower-shaped bead on the cord. Cross the ends in the seed bead on the opposite side of the flower, then thread them through the nearest bicones.

3. Thread three bicones on to the left cord and cross the other end in the last bicone. Thread the top end into the two outer bicones.

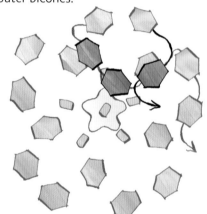

4. Add two bicones to the inner cord and cross the other end in your last bicone. Thread the outer end into the two bicones. Repeat twice. Thread the outer cord into the three bicones at the top, then cross the two ends in a new bicone.

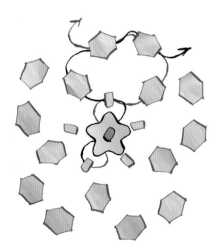

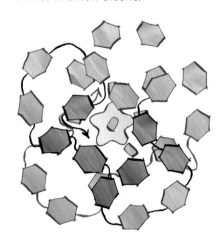

5. Thread the two ends of cord into the bicones in the centre, adding a seed bead between each one. Next, thread the ends into the bicones as indicated in the diagram, then make up your ring base (see page 6). Finish off your ring by following the instructions on page 6.

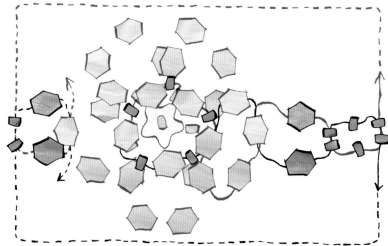

To make this bracelet…

… you will need:

- 38 flower-shaped beads in white
- 14 x 6mm (¹/₄in) faceted beads in turquoise
- 2 x 4mm (⁵/₃₂in) faceted beads in turquoise
- 4 x 3mm (¹/₈in) faceted beads in turquoise
- seed beads in yellow
- 2 bead tips and jewellery glue
- 1 jump ring and 1 clasp
- 1m (40in) nylon cord
- all-purpose pliers

Makes a 15cm (6in) bracelet (minus clasp).

Bracelet

1. Attach a bead tip to a seed bead centred on the cord (see page 7). Work with both ends together to add strength to the bracelet. Thread on a flower (step 2, page 18), two 3mm (¹/₈in) faceted beads, a flower, seed bead, flower and a 4mm (⁵/₃₂in) faceted bead.

2. Next, add a flower, seed bead, flower and a 6mm (¹/₄in) faceted bead. Repeat this motif six times. When you reach the middle of your bracelet, attach four flowers, adding a seed bead between each one.

Tip: completely out of 3mm (¹/₈in) faceted beads? Use 4mm (⁵/₃₂in) faceted beads instead.

3. Thread on a 6mm (¹/₄in) faceted bead, a flower, seed bead and flower. Repeat six times. Add a 4mm (⁵/₃₂in) faceted bead, a flower, seed bead, flower, two 3mm (¹/₈in) faceted beads and a flower. Attach the second bead tip, then add the jump ring and clasp (see page 7).

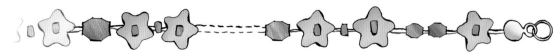

Hair band

1. Work with the cord double to add strength to your design. Thread the band into the centre of the two ends. Add a faceted bead to each end, then cross the ends in another faceted bead.

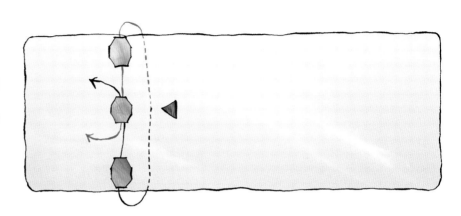

2. Using the technique described in step 2 on page 18, add a flower, faceted bead, flower and a faceted bead to each end of the cord.

Cross the ends in another faceted bead.

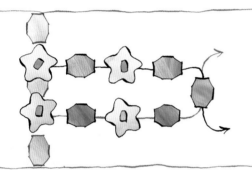

To make this hair band...

... you will need:

- 6 flower-shaped beads in white
- 6 seed beads in yellow
- 10 x 4mm (^{5}/$_{32}$in) faceted beads in turquoise
- 1 hair band
- 1 beading needle
- 2 x 50cm (20in) nylon cord
- all-purpose pliers

3. Add a flower and a faceted bead to each end. Knot the ends on the reverse of the hair band. Then thread two ends of the nylon cord on to a beading needle and sew a few stitches along the band, then trim off the excess. Do the same with the two other ends.

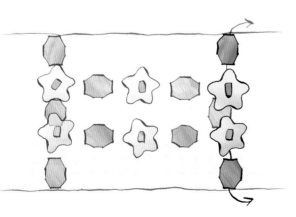

Boiled sweets

A fusion of sweets and stylishness, this brightly coloured bracelet looks good enough to eat.

1. Thread three green seed beads into the centre of the cord and thread it twice through the loop in the clasp. Add another three green seed beads and cross the ends in an orange faceted bead. Thread a green seed bead and a peach faceted bead on to each end, then cross the ends in an orange faceted bead. Repeat this step once, without adding seed beads this time. Thread a peach faceted bead on to each end, then cross the ends in an orange faceted bead.

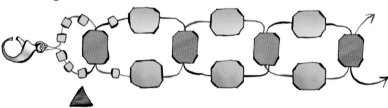

2. Thread both ends into the first hole in a green button and bring them out on top. Thread four orange seed beads on to one end and go back through the first seed bead. Bring the cord out in the second hole in the button and thread it into the faceted bead in the centre. Do the same with the other end of cord.

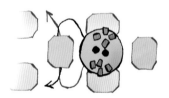

3. Thread the two ends through the hole in the button again and bring them out on top. Add three green seed beads to each end, thread them back through the second hole in the button and cross them in the faceted bead on the right.

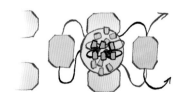

4. Thread two peach faceted beads on to each end and cross them in an orange faceted bead. Repeat twice.

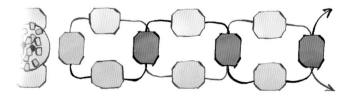

5. To make up the orange buttons, follow steps 2 and 3 but reverse the colours of the seed beads. Repeat step 4. Continue to work in this way until your bracelet is the right size.

6. Finish off by adding two peach faceted beads on to each end of the cord and cross them in an orange faceted bead. Next, thread on orange faceted beads to make the ends of the bracelet the same, using the diagram as a guide. Add three green seed beads to each cord and thread them through the jump ring and back into the seed beads until you reach the two horizontal faceted beads. Thread the ends through all the other faceted beads, adding a green seed bead between each one. Finish off (see page 7).

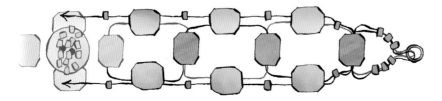

Roses

Be bold and mix materials! Combine glass beads with a metal rose. Why not use these roses in your own designs?

1. Thread a cat's eye bead into the centre of the cord and thread on the other beads as shown in the diagram.

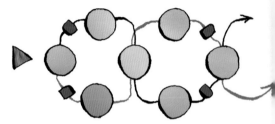

2. Thread a fuchsia seed bead on to each end of the cord and cross the ends in a heart. Thread a fuchsia seed bead on to each end and cross them in the cat's eye bead in the centre. Add a fuchsia seed bead and the rose to the top cord (see step 2, page 18 for instructions) and then another fuchsia seed bead. Thread this end back through the cat's eye bead in the centre.

3. Add four fuchsia seed beads and the heart as shown in the diagram, then cross the ends of cord in the cat's eye bead on the left. Thread the ends so they cross in the right cat's eye bead, adding a round white bead in the centre. Thread a white round bead on to each end and make up the ring base (see page 6). Finish off your ring by following the instructions on page 6.

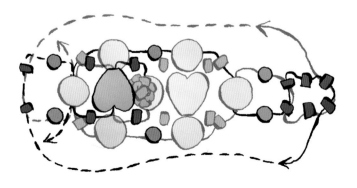

Marbles

These beads are as round as marbles and crystal-clear. The set will add an elegant touch to your everyday wear.

Pendant

1. Thread four green beads into the centre of the cord, then cross the ends in the last bead. Add a white bead to each end and cross the ends in a third white bead. Thread a green bead on to each end, then cross the ends in a white bead. Add two white beads and cross the ends in a green bead. Thread on three more green beads and cross the ends in the last bead.

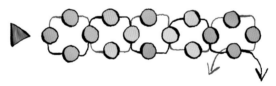

2. Add three green beads to the right cord and cross the ends in the last bead. Thread the upper cord into the bead in the centre. Thread two white beads on to the lower cord and cross the ends in the second bead. Continue to work in this way until you get to the end of the row, using the colours in the diagram as a guide.

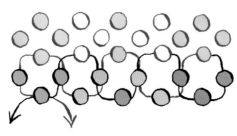

3. Repeat the previous motif, using the diagram below as a guide.

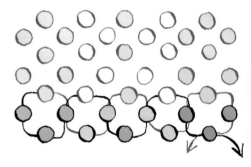

4. In the diagram below the beads are shown face on. The pale beads represent the first and last rows that you made up in steps 1 to 3. The coloured beads are the last side of your bead rectangle joining these rows together. Using the diagram as a guide, thread the nylon cord into the pale beads and cross the ends in the coloured beads.

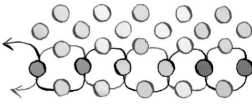

5. Knot your cords and finish off (see page 6). Thread the satin cord through the tube of beads and attach leather crimps, clasp and jump rings (see page 7).

Pendant cross-section

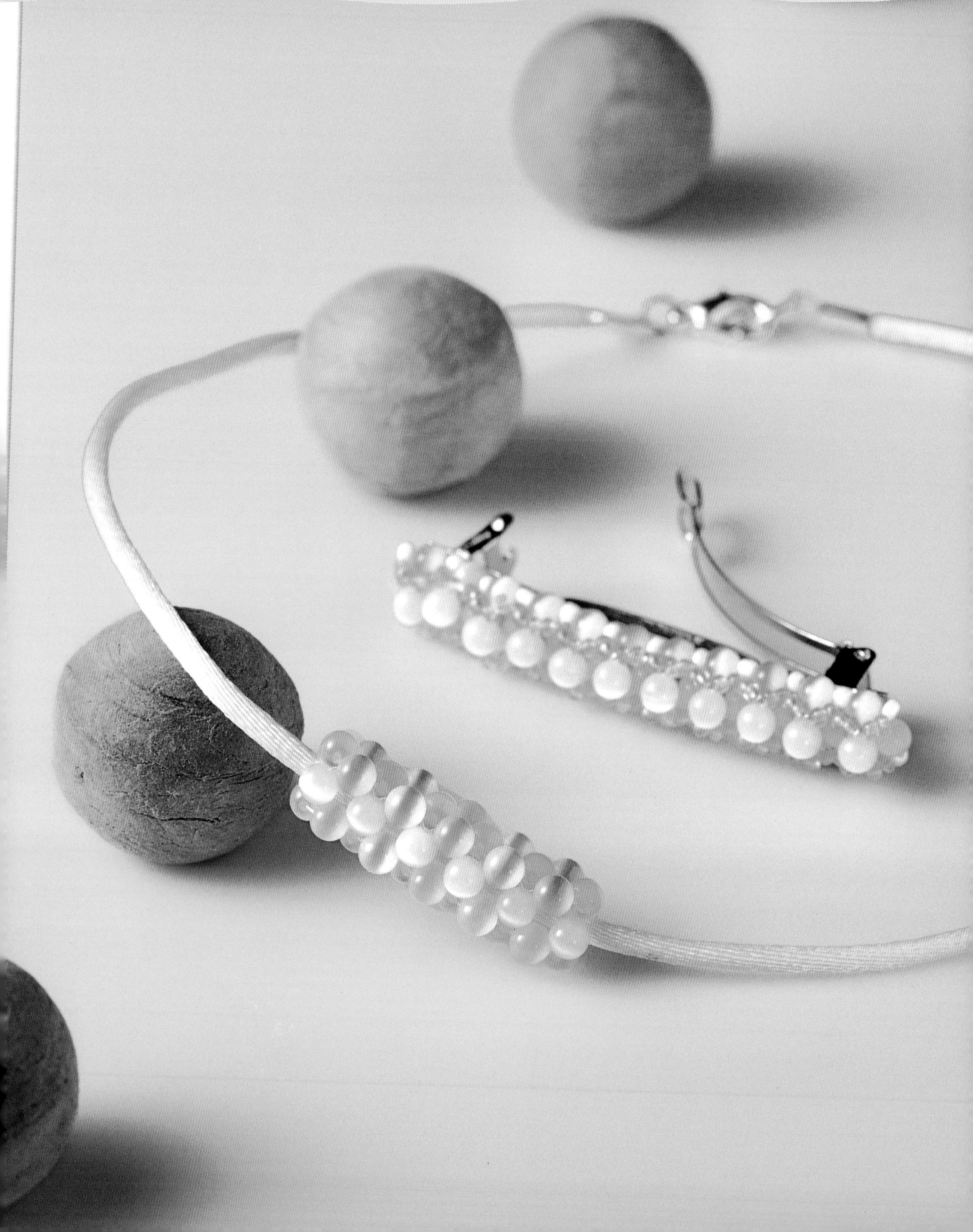

Ring

1. Thread a green bead into the centre of the cord. Add a white bead to the left and a green bead to the right and cross the ends in a third green bead. Add a bead to either side, a white bead on the left and a green bead on the right, then cross the ends in a green bead. Repeat this motif three more times.

Thread a bead in the right colour on to each end, then cross the ends in your starter green bead.

3. Here the design is shown looking down on your work. Thread the ends through the white beads until you have crossed them.

4. Thread two green seed beads on to each end, then thread the ends together into a green bead. Thread two green seed beads on to each end of cord. Cross them in the white bead opposite the bead you started from.

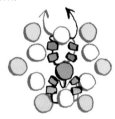

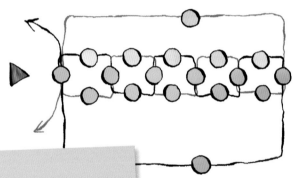

2. This diagram shows how your work should look sideways on. Thread your ends into the beads and bring them out in the white cat's eye bead at the top.

5. Thread your ends of cord into the green beads, adding two white seed beads between each one. Cross them in the bottom bead, make up your ring base and finish off (see page 6).

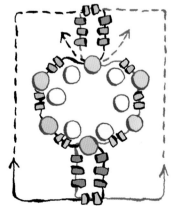

Hairslide

1. Start by making up the base. Thread on three green beads and cross the ends in a fourth bead. Add a green bead on to each end of the cord and cross them in another green bead. Repeat this motif a further nine times.

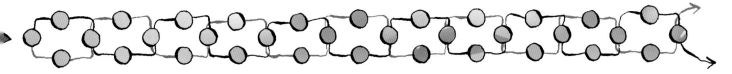

2. Thread two green seed beads on to each end of the cord and cross the ends in a white bead. Add another two green seed beads to each end. Cross the ends in the first central green bead. Continue to work in this way until you have added 11 white beads.

3. Thread the ends of cord back through the green beads along the sides, adding a white seed bead between each one. Cross the ends in the last green bead. Finish off (see page 6). Add a little glue to the hairslide mount and place your beadwork on top.

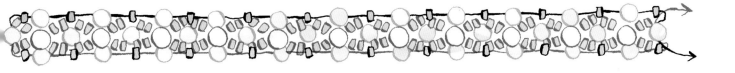

He loves me, he loves me not

He may or may not love you, but you will adore this ring. Make sure your sister doesn't pinch it!

1. Thread a seed bead into the centre of the copper wire, thread the two ends of wire into a heart-shaped bead, then add a seed bead to each end.

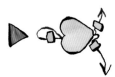

2. Add a heart-shaped bead and a seed bead to your top wire, go back through the heart and add another seed bead. Keep the wire nice and tight. Repeat this motif once more on this wire and three times on the other wire. Finish by crossing the two ends in a seed bead.

3. Thread a seed bead on to each end of the wire, then thread the two ends into a 6mm (¹⁄₄in) faceted bead and add another seed bead to each end. Thread one end into the seed bead at the centre, through the heart and into the seed bead at the

top of the heart. Go back through the heart, keeping the wire tight, and trim off the excess. Do the same with the other end of wire.

4. Thread the nylon cord into a seed bead in the centre and make up your ring base (see page 6). Use the instructions given on that page to finish off.

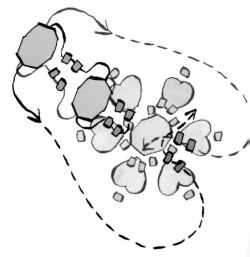

Petal ring

A delicate and slender design. For a formal occasion opt for iridescent beads; for going out with friends, choose the fuchsia ring.

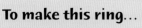

To make this ring…

… you will need:

- 1 flower-shaped bead in white
- seed beads in iridescent blue
- 60cm (24in) nylon cord
- all-purpose pliers

1. Thread six seed beads into the centre of the cord and thread the cord back through the first seed bead. Thread the two ends into the flower-shaped bead and cross them in a seed bead. Add three seed beads to one end and thread it back through the first seed bead. Thread the other end through all these beads. Bring the two ends out together under the flower and cross them in the seed bead at the opposite end.

2. Turn your work over so your flower is face down. Thread ten seed beads on to the left cord and thread it back through the first seed bead. Thread the end into the seed bead in the centre. Add six seed beads and thread the cord back through the first five seed beads. Repeat the whole process from the start. Finish with a loop of ten seed beads, then thread the cord into the seed bead in the centre.

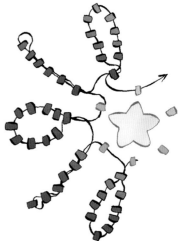

3. Use the right end to make three stalks and three loops in the same way, going through the seed beads in the centre, as indicated in the diagram.

This version of the ring is made with fuchsia seed beads. Why not alter the number of seed beads on the stalks and loops on both models to suit your taste?

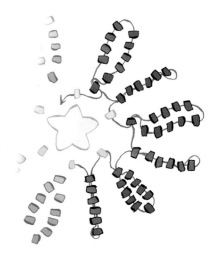

4. Thread the left cord into the next seed bead, then make up your ring base and finish off (see page 6).

Tip: you can vary the design by increasing or decreasing the number of 'petals' on your flower.

Morning dew

These delicate green and yellow beads are like drops of morning dew. Add a butterfly clasp for a romantic bracelet for a young dreamer.

1. Take two lengths of thread and tie three knots one over the other to fix the centre of the bracelet. Thread on the beads, using the diagram as a guide. Tie three knots between each group of three beads to secure them on the thread.

2. Do the same with the other two threads to attach the remaining beads.

To make this bracelet…

… you will need:

- 10 chip beads in green
- 23 round opaque beads in yellow
- 4mm ($^5/_{32}$in) miracle beads: 6 yellow and 6 green
- 6mm ($^1/_4$in) miracle beads: 6 yellow and 6 green
- 2 costume beads (yellow butterflies) for the clasp
- 4 x 25cm (10in) extra strong sewing thread
- pin and beading needle
- all-purpose pliers

Makes a 16cm (6$^1/_4$in) bracelet (minus clasp).

3. When choosing the costume beads for the clasp (butterflies were used here), make sure the hole is large enough to accommodate all your threads. Thread the butterflies side by side on to the four ends. Add a 6mm ($^1/_4$in) round yellow bead to the four top threads at each end, then tie knots at the ends to secure the beads, leaving enough thread so you can put your bracelet over your wrist. To tighten your bracelet around your wrist, simply pull on the two large round yellow beads. Divide the remaining threads into pairs and add a 4mm ($^5/_{32}$in) round yellow bead to each end.

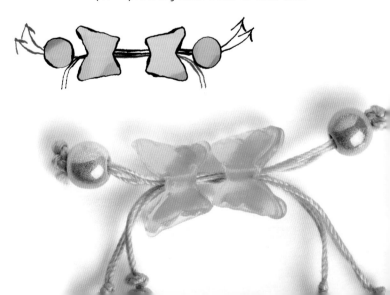

Tip: because the thread is very flexible, use a beading needle to thread on the chips and beads. This will make it much easier. Use the pin to clear the holes in your chip beads, which are often poorly finished.

Total diva

Make up this bracelet, ring and Alice band and you will look like a fairytale princess. You might even meet your Prince Charming...

Bracelet

1. Thread nine seed beads into the centre of the cord, then cross the ends in another seed bead. Thread one of the ends back through the beads to strengthen the clasp ring. Using the colours in the diagram as a guide, add seed beads and round beads.

2. Add the centre beads, then cross the ends in the round bead on the left. Thread the ends through the outer beads and cross them in the round bead on the right.

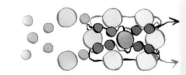

3. Add four seed beads, two dark round beads and six light round beads as shown in the diagram.

4. Repeat the motifs in steps 2 and 3 until your bracelet is the correct size. To finish off the clasp, add seed beads and round beads on to each end, then bring the cords together in a round bead and a seed bead.

5. Thread both ends into the first round bead together and add four seed beads on to each side. Thread the ends through some beads until they meet and then finish off (see page 7).

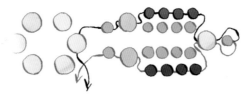

To make this ring…

… you will need:

- 7 x 4mm (⁵/₃₂in) round light-coloured mother-of-pearl beads
- 2 x 4mm (⁵/₃₂in) round dark-coloured mother-of-pearl beads
- seed beads in bronze
- 50cm (20in) nylon cord
- all-purpose pliers

Ring

1. Attach the seven light-coloured beads as shown in the diagram.

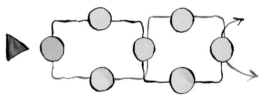

2. Add two seed beads to each of the ends and cross them in a dark-coloured round bead. Thread another two seed beads on to each end of the cord and cross them in the round bead in the centre. Repeat this motif once.

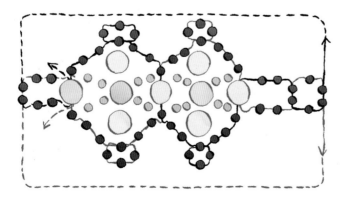

3. Add seven seed beads to the top end and thread it back through the fourth bead. Thread on three seed beads and thread the cord into the round bead in the centre. Do the same with the other end. Thread each end back through the seed bead next to the centre round bead. Add six seed beads to the top cord and thread it back through the third seed bead. Add three seed beads and thread the end into the round bead on the right. Repeat with the other end of the cord. Make up the ring base and follow the instructions on page 6 to finish off.

Alice band

1. Using the diagram as a guide, thread 14 light-coloured round beads on to the 50cm (20in) cord.

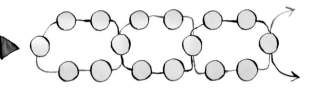

2. To make up the underside of the base, use the technique detailed in step 2 of the ring on page 38.

3. Thread three round beads on to the lower cord with four seed beads between each one, then thread on a final seed bead. Thread the end back into the round bead. To finish the end, make a loop around the strand of beads, slide the end into the loop and tighten the knot so it sits above the round bead. Tie another knot, then slip the end into the beads for at least 1cm (³/₈in). Use this technique to finish off all of the ends. Thread 20 seed beads, a round bead and a seed bead on to the other end of the cord and go back through the round bead. In the diagram each stalk is made from a separate length of cord.

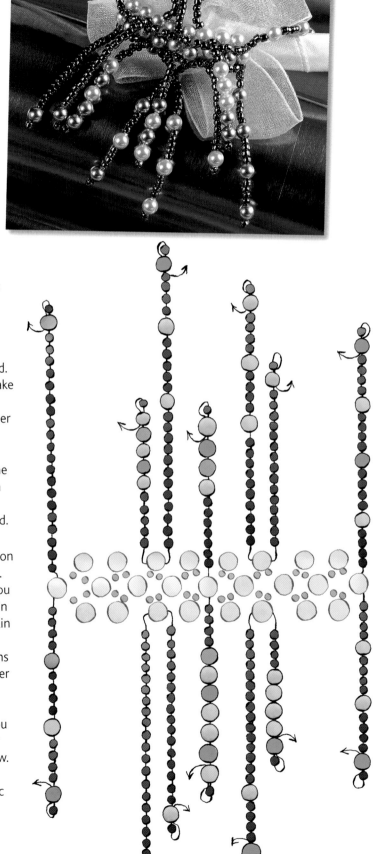

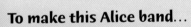

To make this Alice band…

… you will need:

- 47 x 4mm (⁵/₃₂in) light-coloured mother-of-pearl beads
- 23 x 4mm (⁵/₃₂in) dark-coloured mother-of-pearl beads
- seed beads in bronze
- 2 x 16cm (6¹/₄in) muslin ribbon 2cm (³/₄in) wide
- 60cm (24in) satin ribbon 1.5cm (⁵/₈in) wide
- needle and thread
- fabric glue and jewellery glue
- 1 plastic Alice band
- 50cm (20in) nylon cord
- 6 x 20cm (8in) strands nylon cord 0.25mm (30 gauge) diameter
- all-purpose pliers

4. Wrap the satin ribbon around the Alice band. Apply fabric glue as you go. Stitch across to join the ends of each muslin ribbon to make two loops. Place the ribbons one on top of the other and wind a length of sewing thread around them in the centre. You should now have four ribbon loops like a bow. Attach them to the Alice band using fabric glue and fix the bead design on top with jewellery glue.

Pyramid

You can make up this sparkling pyramid ring in different colourways.

To make this ring...

... you will need:

- 12 x 4mm (5/32in) cat's eye beads in yellow
- about 15 x 4mm (5/32in) faceted beads in green
- seed beads in green and yellow
- 60cm (24in) nylon cord
- all-purpose pliers

1. Thread on four cat's eye beads and a seed bead and go back through the first cat's eye bead.

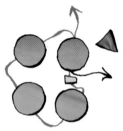

2. Add three cat's eye beads to the outer end and a seed bead to the inner end and cross them in your last cat's eye bead. Repeat once. Thread two cat's eye beads on to the outer end and a seed bead on to the inner end and cross them in your starter cat's eye bead.

3. Thread your lower end into the cat's eye on the left and cross your cords in a seed bead, a faceted bead and a seed bead. Tighten. Thread the lower end into the next two cat's eyes, adding a seed bead between them.

4. Repeat the motif in step 3 three times. Finish by threading the inner end into your starter seed beads and faceted beads. Cross the ends in the cat's eye bead at the bottom.

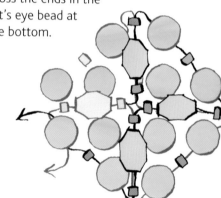

5. Thread the ends through the round beads on the outside, adding a seed bead in the places indicated in the diagram. Cross the ends in a seed bead, make up the ring base and follow the instructions on page 6 to finish.

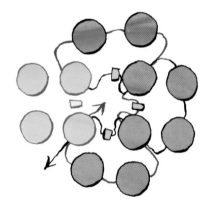

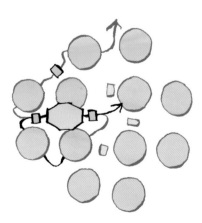

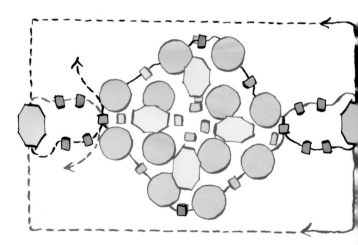

Ribbon of beads

To make this bracelet...

... you will need:

- about 25 x 4mm (⁵/₃₂in) faceted beads in silver
- about 25 x 4mm (⁵/₃₂in) faceted beads in green
- seed beads in green
- 2 x 20cm (8in) satin cord
- 2 large bead tips
- jewellery glue
- 1 jump ring
- 1 clasp
- clear nail varnish
- 2 x 15cm (6in) copper wire
- 0.18mm (32 gauge) in diameter
- 2 x 25cm (10in) nylon cord
- 4 x 10cm (4in) nylon cord
- all-purpose pliers

Makes a 15cm (6in) bracelet (minus clasp).

If you like mixing materials you will love this bracelet with its beads interwoven with satin cord.

1. Tie two double knots to join the two 25cm (10in) lengths of nylon cord together and apply a little clear nail varnish to the knots. Thread the seed beads and faceted beads on to each cord, using the diagram below as a guide.

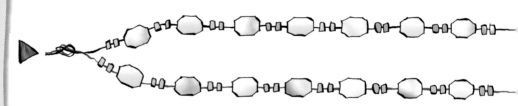

2. To attach the clasp to the bead tips, thread the clasp on to a doubled-up 10cm (4in) length of nylon cord. Thread the four ends into one of the bead tips. Add a seed bead to two of the ends and tie three knots. Add some nail varnish. Leave to dry and trim the excess. Do the same with the other bead tip, adding the jump ring instead this time.

3. Place the ends of the two satin cords and the two beaded nylon cords together. Wind copper wire very tightly around them, just above the knots. Twist the wire around several times before trimming the excess. Flatten with pliers. Apply jewellery glue to the bead tip, place the wired end of your bracelet inside and close the two shells with the pliers.

4. Keep the two strings of beads in the centre and start with the two lengths of satin cord on the outside. Thread the two lengths of satin cord under each string of beads towards the centre, cross them and thread them over each string of beads.

Tip: after threading on all your beads, put a clip on the end of the nylon cords to stop your beads coming off. This will make it easier to weave in your satin cord.

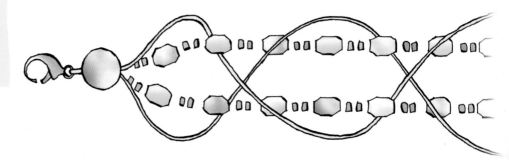

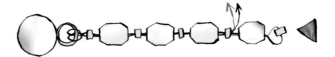

Work all the way along the bracelet in this way. Try it out for size on your wrist, remembering to take the clasp and bead tips into account. At this stage it isn't too late to make the bracelet shorter. Attach the second bead tip using the technique in step 3.

5. Thread a seed bead into the centre of one of the remaining 10cm (4in) lengths of nylon cord. Thread the two ends of the cord into a silver faceted bead then alternate seed beads and faceted beads to the

end. Wind the cord twice around the clasp jump ring, then thread it back through the beads to the other end. Tie a knot in the ends and finish off (see page 6).

Use the same technique to make up the second tail of beads, this time attaching it to the clasp ring.

Sleeping Beauty

Make up this delicate jewellery which is fit for a sleeping princess and wear it with your favourite dress.

To make this pendant...

... you will need:

- 9 x 7mm (⁹/₃₂in) clear wheel beads
- 8 x 7mm (⁹/₃₂in) wheel beads in pink
- seed beads in pale pink
- 40cm (16in) satin ribbon
- 2 leather crimps and a clasp
- 1 small and 1 large jump ring
- 60cm (24in) nylon cord
- all-purpose pliers

Pendant

1. Thread a pink wheel bead into the centre of the cord, then thread on seed beads and clear wheels as shown in the diagram. Cross the ends in a pink wheel and add a seed bead on to each end.

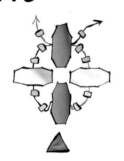

2. Add a pink wheel, two seed beads, a clear wheel, two seed beads, a pink wheel, two seed beads, a clear wheel and two seed beads on to the left end. Thread the end back through the pink wheel and add a seed bead. Do the same with the right end.

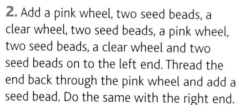

3. Cross the two ends in a pink wheel. Add seed beads and clear wheels on to each end and cross them in a pink wheel.

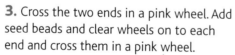

4. To make the loop for the pendant, thread five seed beads on to each end, cross them in a clear wheel, add a further five seed beads and cross them in the pink wheel. Finish off (see page 7).

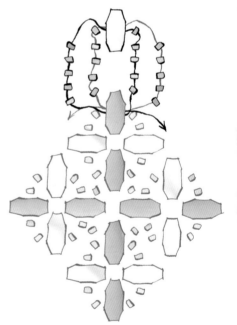

5. Thread the pendant on to the satin ribbon and check the length. Attach leather crimps, jump rings and a clasp to the ribbon as described on page 7.

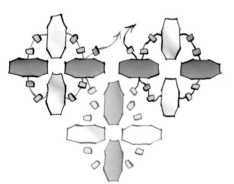

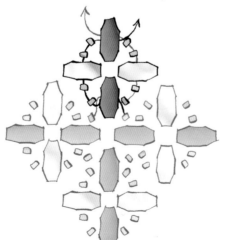

Earrings

1. Thread a clear wheel bead into the centre of the cord. Add two seed beads on to the right end and three on to the left end. Add a clear wheel on each side. Thread two seed beads on to the left end and three on to the right end, then cross the ends in a clear wheel.

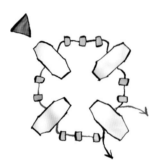

2. Add two seed beads, a pink wheel and two seed beads to the lower cord. Go through the clear wheel bead. Repeat this process once on each end of cord. Thread two seed beads on to each end of cord and cross them in a pink wheel.

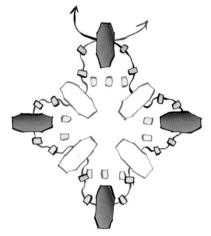

3. Thread three seed beads on to each end and cross the ends in the loop in your earring mount. Add two seed beads to each end and cross them behind the earring mount. Thread the ends back through the two seed beads, then finish off (see page 7).

Make up the second earring in exactly the same way.

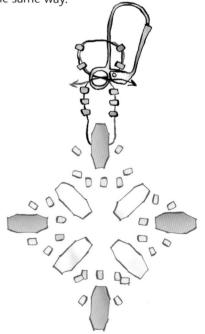

Ring

1. Thread four faceted beads on to the nylon cord and cross the end through the first faceted bead.

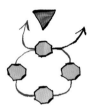

2. Add two seed beads, a pink wheel, a seed bead, a clear wheel and two seed beads to the left end and thread the cord through the faceted bead at the bottom. Repeat this motif with the other end, but adding the wheel bead colours in reverse this time.

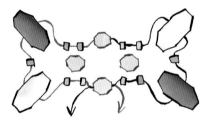

3. Add two seed beads, a clear wheel, three seed beads, a clear wheel and two seed beads to the left end and through the faceted bead at the top. Thread two seed beads and a pink wheel on to the other end, go into the seed bead in the centre, add another pink wheel and two seed beads and through the faceted bead in the centre.

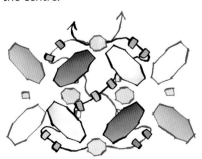

To make this ring…

… you will need:

- 8 x 7mm (⁹⁄₃₂in) clear wheel beads
- 4 x 7mm (⁹⁄₃₂in) wheel beads in pink
- 4 x 4mm (⁵⁄₃₂in) faceted, clear beads
- seed beads in pale pink
- 60cm (24in) nylon cord
- all-purpose pliers

4. Add a clear wheel and two seed beads to each end of the cord and cross the ends in two more seed beads. Continue all the way around the ring until it is the right size. To finish, add a clear wheel on to each end of the cord and cross them in the faceted bead at the bottom. Finish off (see page 6).

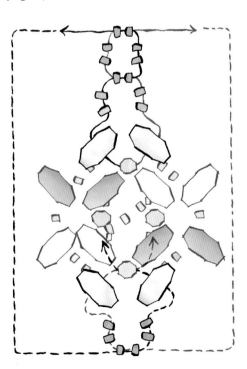

Indian summer

Hot late summer shades blend to make this delightful floral necklace.

To make this necklace…

… you will need:

- about 70 x 4mm (⁵/₃₂in) glass bicones in pink
- about 40 chip beads in ochre
- micro bugle beads in pink
- seed beads in orange
- 1 barrel clasp
- 2 x 2m (2¹/₄yd) silver-plated copper wire 0.18mm (32 gauge) in diameter
- all-purpose pliers

1. Thread the clasp into the centre of one of the lengths of wire. Wind the two ends around each other fairly tightly for about 1cm (³/₈in). Add the loops (see step 2), twisting the wires as you go. At the centre of the necklace, make a loop with four beads, then continue as before. When you get to the end, cross the ends of the wire in the ring of the other half of the clasp and wind them tightly around each other. Trim any excess wire.

2. To make up the loops thread three different beads on to one end of wire, leaving a little excess wire, then twist the wire around on itself until it meets the other wire. Continue winding the two wires together until you reach the position for the next loop. Make the next loop out of the longer end of wire.

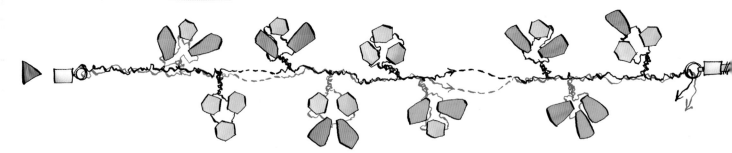

Tip: alternate between ochre chip beads and glass bicones on the loops. Use the loops in the diagrams for inspiration, or simply get creative and go with the flow!

3. Thread the other length of wire through the ring of the clasp so the clasp is in the centre and wind it around your beaded wire for 1cm (³/₈in). Thread micro bugles all the way along one end of the wire and then wind it around your necklace. Thread seed beads on to the other end of wire and wind it over the top. Finish off as described at the end of step 1.

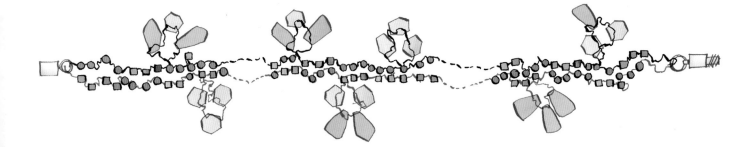

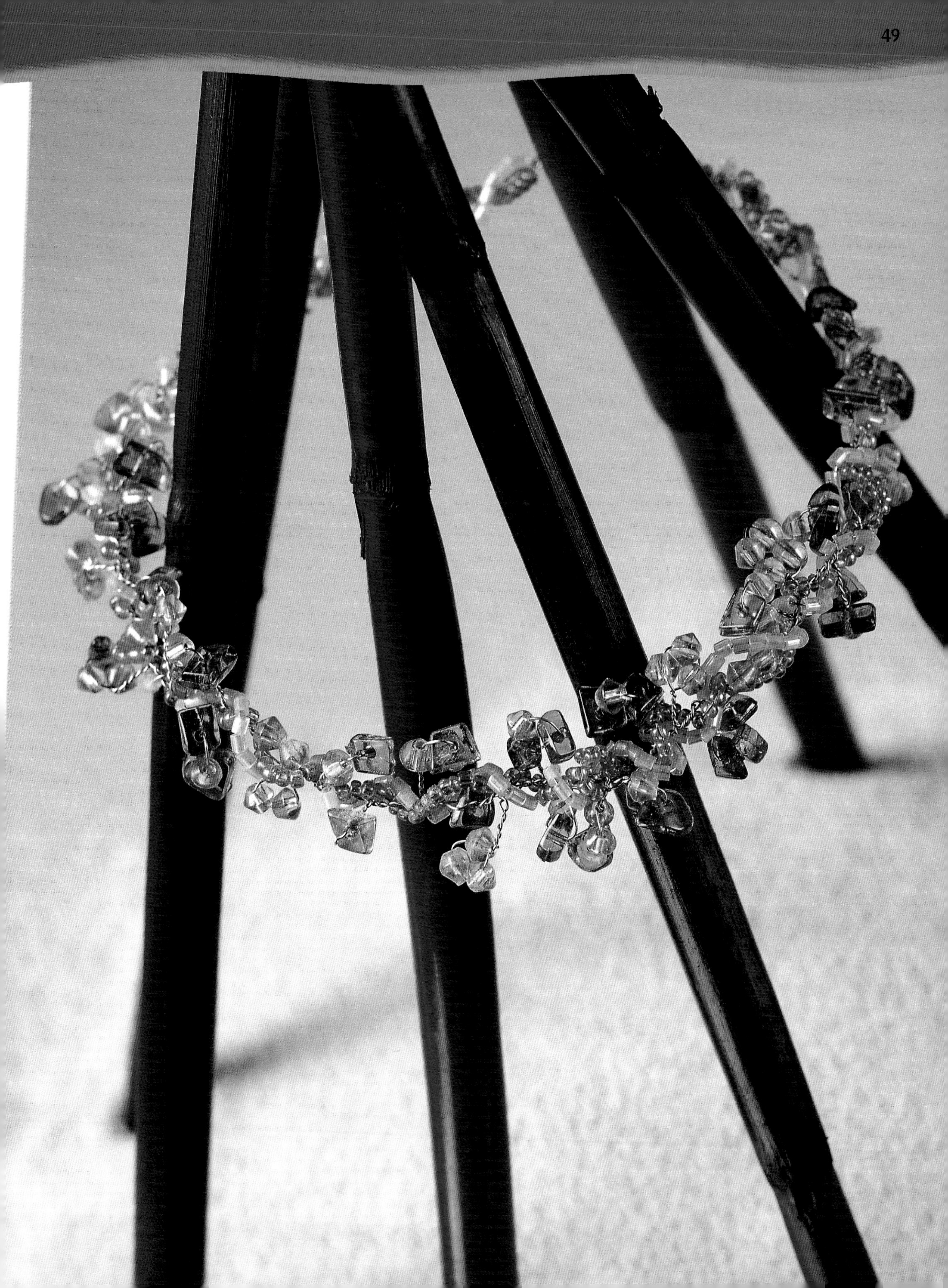

On the banks of the Nile

A classic piece revisited just for you. Perfect for all ages.

To make this ring…

… you will need:

- 3 x 4mm ($^{5}/_{32}$in) round satin mother-of-pearl beads
- 12 x 3mm ($^{1}/_{8}$in) large seed beads in royal blue
- about 8 x 3mm ($^{1}/_{8}$in) faceted beads in royal blue for the ring base
- seed beads in royal blue
- 50cm (20in) nylon cord
- all-purpose pliers

1. Thread five large seed beads on to the centre of the cord and add two small seed beads on either side. Cross the ends in three mother-of-pearl beads and two large seed beads as shown in the diagram.

2. Thread two small seed beads on to each end, then cross them in five large seed beads.

3. Thread the left end through all the beads on the outside, then cross both the ends in the seed beads on the right.

4. Make up the ring base (see page 6) and follow the instructions on page 7 to finish off.

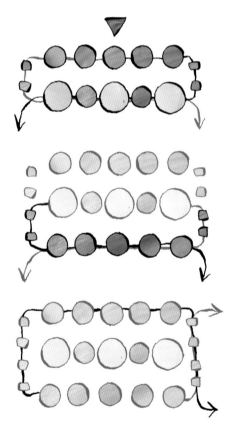

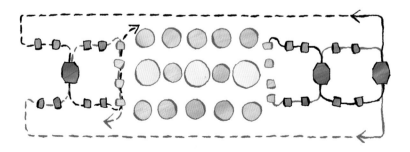

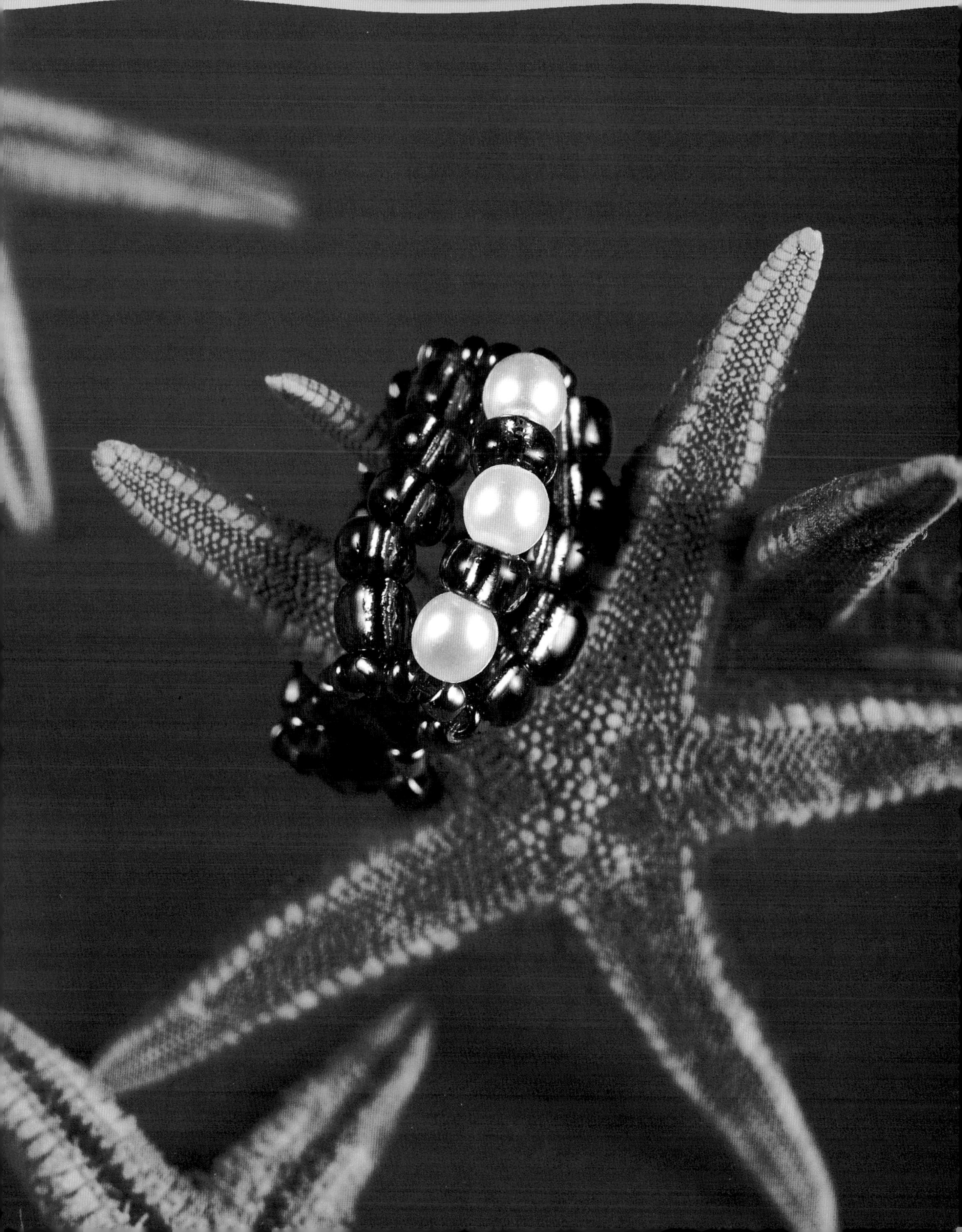

Futuristic

A truly modern ring with geometric shapes and a delicate touch in the centre to liven up your outfit.

To make this ring...

... you will need:

- 1 metal rose in royal blue
- 6 x 3mm (1/8in) large seed beads in royal blue
- 16 bugle beads in silver
- seed beads in yellow and royal blue
- 60cm (24in) nylon cord
- all-purpose pliers

1. Thread three bugles into the centre of the cord, then thread one end back through the first bugle.

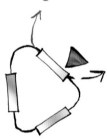

2. Thread two bugles on to the outer cord and cross the other end in the second bugle. Repeat this process three more times. Add a bugle to the outer cord, then thread both ends into the starter bugle.

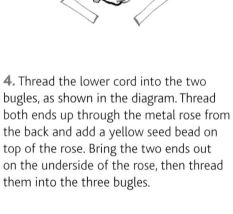

4. Thread the lower cord into the two bugles, as shown in the diagram. Thread both ends up through the metal rose from the back and add a yellow seed bead on top of the rose. Bring the two ends out on the underside of the rose, then thread them into the three bugles.

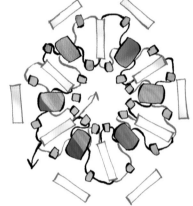

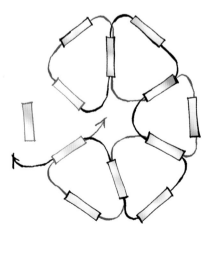

3. To make up the top of the ring, thread a yellow seed bead on to each end and cross the ends in a large blue seed bead. Repeat this process five more times.

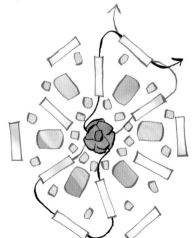

5. Thread the left cord into all the bugles on the outside, adding a yellow seed bead between each one, until you get to the bugle on the right. Add a yellow seed bead on to the right cord, then thread it into the next bugle. Thread a bugle on to each end and start to make up your ring base (see page 6), alternating between yellow and blue seed beads as you go.

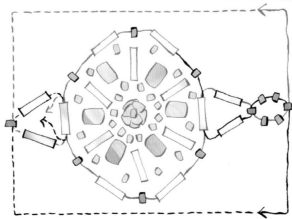

Ring of romance

A delicate ring for true romantics.

1. Thread a mauve faceted bead into the centre of the cord, then thread a seed bead and a violet faceted bead on to each end and cross them in a seed bead. Thread a mauve faceted bead and a seed bead on to each end and cross them in a violet faceted bead.

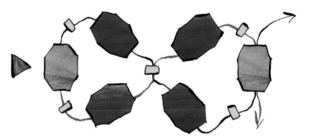

2. To add strength to your ring, thread the cord back through all the beads in step 1 in the opposite direction. Make up the ring base. Thread two seed beads on to each end and cross them in two more seed beads. Continue to work in this way, threading a seed bead on to each end and crossing the ends in two seed beads. Repeat until your ring is the correct size. Finish by threading two seed beads on to each end and crossing the ends in your faceted bead on the left. To get the two ends into the correct position to tie your knots, thread one end through a few beads. Finish off (see page 7).

Tip: why not make up a larger version of this ring? When you get to the end of step 1, add a seed bead on to each end and add a second set of four violet faceted beads. Next, add a seed bead on to each end, then cross them in a mauve faceted bead. Finish off as described in step 2.

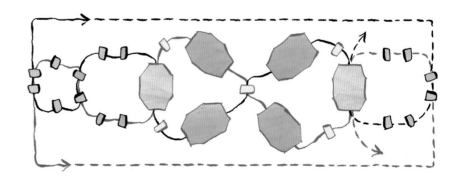

Holiday hairclips

Fancy a new hairstyle? There's no need to go to the hairdresser. Just glam up a simple hairclip with beads.

Miracle bead hairclip

1. In this step, each group of beads comprises two 4mm (⁵/32in) miracle beads in different colours and a seed bead in the centre. Thread your first group of beads into the centre of your wire, thread the two ends round the back of your clip and wind them together (1). Add your other beads in the same way, following the numbers (2, 3, 4) in the diagram.

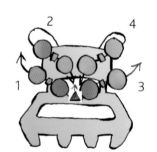

2. Bring the two ends of wire round to the front and cross them in a 6mm (¹/4in) green bead. Using the diagram as a guide, add beads to one end and thread the end back into the two round beads at the top. Tighten and repeat on the other end of the wire.

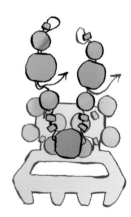

3. Thread one end of wire through to the front and slide it under the green bead. Thread on a 6mm (¹/4in) yellow bead and a seed bead. Wind the two wires on to the back of the clip, then trim the excess.

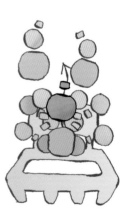

Spring hairclip

1. Attach a flower and a small leaf to the front of your clip, winding the metal stalks around the hairclip. Do the same with the large leaf, this time attaching it to the back of the clip.

2. Thread on cat's eye beads and seed beads to cover the clip. Go back through some existing beads. Make a seed bead loop with two cat's eye beads on the top so that it sticks out above the clip. Wind the ends of your wire around the back, then trim the excess.

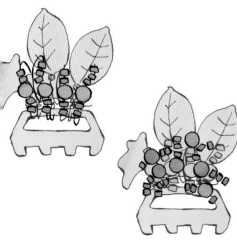

To make this hairclip…

… you will need:

- 1 hairclip
- 1 yellow flower on metal stalk
- 1 large and 1 small yellow leaf on metal stalk
- about 12 x 4mm ($^5/_{32}$in) cat's eye beads in yellow
- seed beads in green
- 60cm (24in) thin copper wire 0.18mm (32 gauge) in diameter
- all-purpose pliers

Queen of the Night

To make this bracelet…

… you will need:

- 36 x faceted olive beads 6 x 4mm ($^1/_4$ x $^5/_{32}$in) in black
- 38 x 4mm ($^5/_{32}$in) faceted beads in black
- seed beads in bright colours
- 2 bead tips
- jewellery glue
- 1 clasp and 1 jump ring
- 2m (2$^1/_4$yd) nylon cord
- all-purpose pliers

Makes a 15.5cm (6$^1/_4$in) bracelet (minus clasp).

Make yourself Queen of the Night in these shimmering pieces.

1. Attach a bead tip to the middle of the cord (see page 7). Thread two seed beads on to each end and cross them in a faceted bead. Now repeat the following motif until you have made up nine triangles in total. Thread a seed bead on to either side then thread a faceted bead and a seed bead on to the lower end and cross the two ends in a faceted bead. Add a seed bead to each end, then add a faceted bead and a seed bead to the upper end and cross the ends in a faceted bead.

2. Thread a seed bead, an olive bead and a seed bead on to each end. Thread the cord back into the olive bead. Repeat this process until you have added 17 olive beads to each cord. Add a seed bead to each end, then cross the ends in a faceted bead. Work the rest of your faceted beads as described in step 1. Finish by adding two seed beads to each end, thread both ends into the second bead tip and attach the clasp (see page 7).

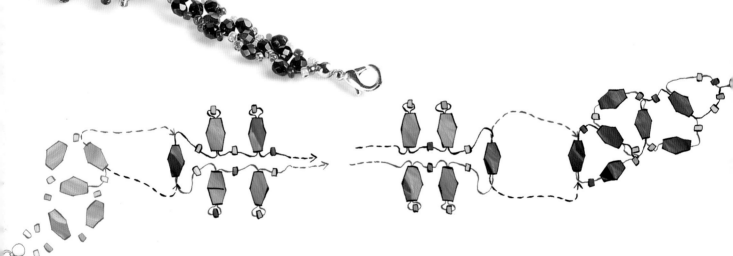

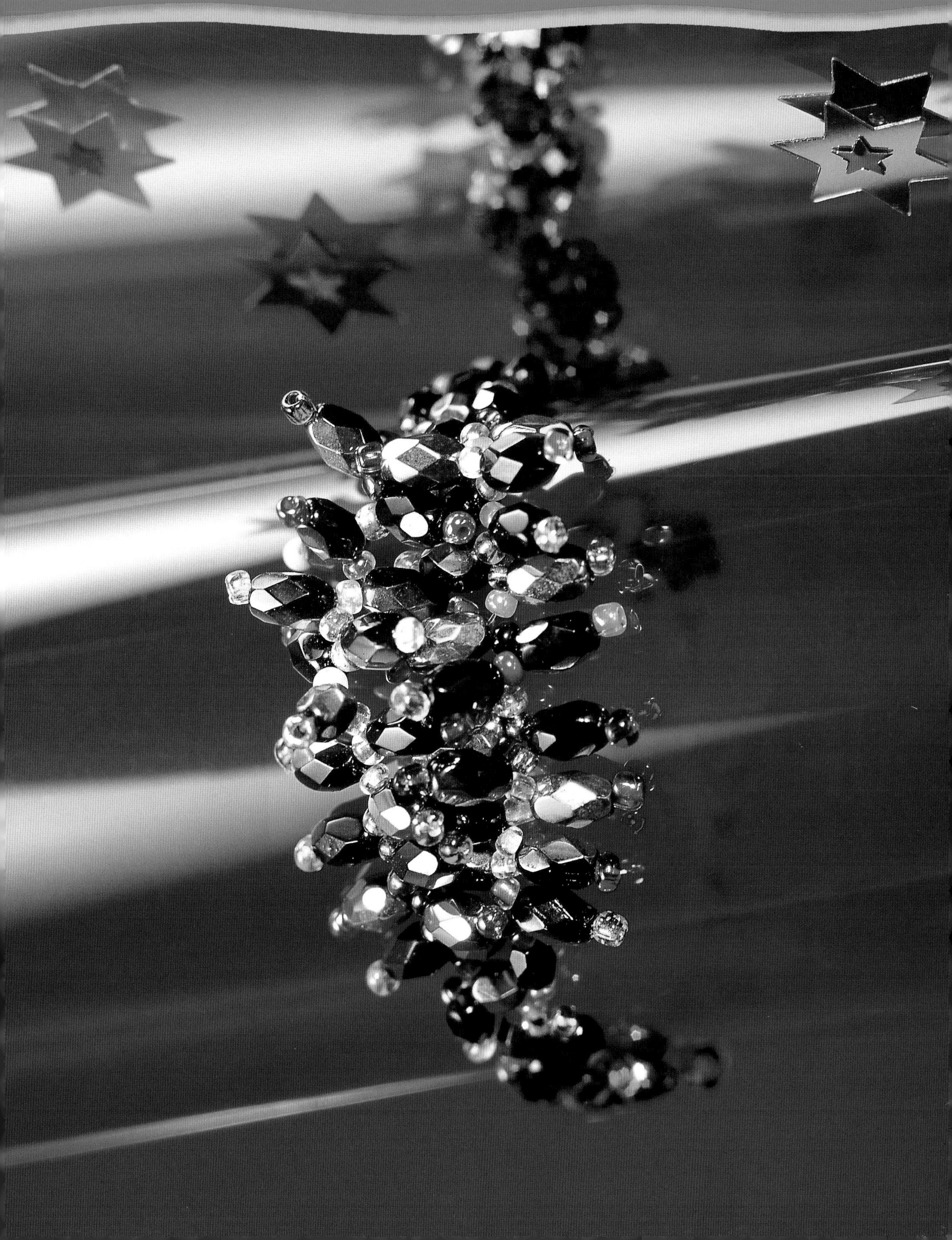

Ring

1. Thread two seed beads into the centre of the cord and add an olive bead and a seed bead on each side. Thread each of the ends back through the olive bead and add another seed bead.

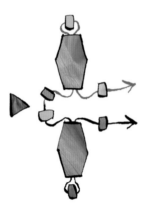

2. Using the same technique as in step 2 of the bracelet, add seven olive beads on to each end with seed beads around each one. To finish, cross the ends in two seed beads. Make up your ring base (see page 6) and finish off (see page 7).

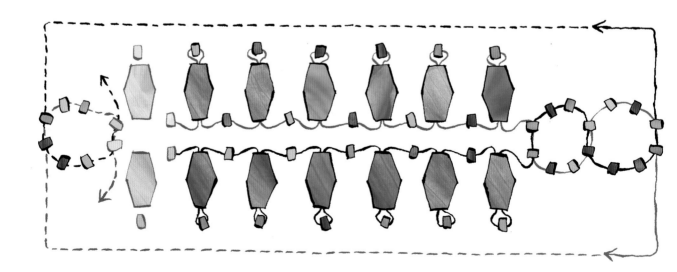

Snow flowers

Bouquets of white flowers make very pretty and very feminine pieces.

Ring

1. Tie a knot in the end of the four cords and make your ring base. Separate the ends into pairs and thread two seed beads on to each pair of ends. Cross the four ends in a faceted bead. Continue to work in this way until your ring is the correct size.

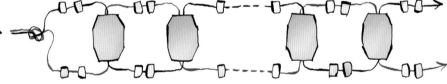

2. Secure the four ends together with several knots. Thread a needle on to each pair of ends. Attach a muslin flower with a few stitches, adding a few seed beads on top. Bring the ends out underneath, tie them in a knot and thread them through a few beads. Trim the excess.

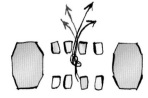

Tip: make the ring first because it is less tricky. This will give you plenty of practice for the hairslide!

Hairslide

1. Thread four seed beads into the centre of the 60cm (24in) cord and cross one of the ends in the first bead. Thread a seed bead on to each end and cross them in another seed bead. Add three seed beads to the left end and cross the right end in the last seed bead.

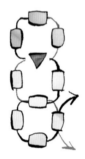

3. Repeat step 2 but work from top to bottom this time. Continue in this way until your design is the same length as your hairslide.

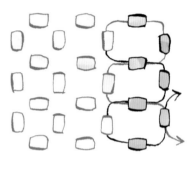

2. Add three seed beads to the lower end and cross the other end in the last seed bead. Thread two seed beads on to the right end, thread the left end through the seed bead in the centre and cross them in the second seed bead. Thread the left end into the seed bead in the centre, add two seed beads and cross the other end in the second seed bead.

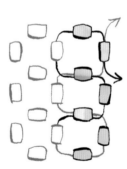

4. Thread each end through all the outer seed beads, adding a seed bead between each one. When the ends meet, tie them in a knot and finish off (see page 7). Thread four seed beads in the centre of one of the 15cm (6in) lengths of cord and cross the ends in the last seed bead. Attach the first muslin flower as described in step 2 of the ring on page 61. Repeat this step to make the two other flowers. Add a drop of clear nail varnish to all your knots and trim the excess once dry. Glue to the hairslide, holding it in place for a few seconds for the glue to take effect.

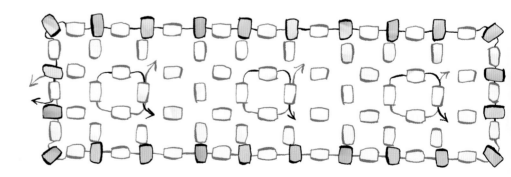

Suppliers

UK

The Bead Shop
7 Market Street
Nottingham NG1 6HY
tel: 00 44 115 9588899
www.mailorder-beads.co.uk

Constellation Beads
The Coach House
Barningham, Richmond
North Yorkshire DL11 7DW
tel: 00 44 1833 621 094
www.constellationbeads.co.uk

Creative Beadcraft Ltd
Unit 2 Asheridge Business Centre
Asheridge Road, Chesham
Buckinghamshire HP5 2PT
tel: 00 44 1494 778 818
www.creativebeadcraft.co.uk

JRM Beads Ltd
16 Redbridge Enterprise Centre
Thompson Close, Ilford
Essex IG1 1TY
tel: 00 44 20 8553 3240
www.beadworks.co.uk

Bead Exclusive
Nixon House
119-121 Teignmouth Road
Torquay
Devon TQ1 4HA
tel: 00 44 1803 322 000
www.bead-exclusive.com

Jilly Beads
29 Hexham Road
Morecombe LA4 6PE
tel: 00 44 1524 412 728
www.jillybeads.com

The Rocking Rabbit Trading Company
7 The Green, Haddenham
Cambridge CB6 3TA
tel: 00 44 870 606 1588
www.rockingrabbit.co.uk

USA

Bangles and Beads
3322 West Cary Street
Richmond VA 232211
tel: 001 804 355 6118
www.banglesandbeads.net

Bead Bar
1319 Edgewater Drive
Orlando FL 32804
tel: 001 407 426 8826
www.beadbar.com

Bead Box Inc.
4860 East Baseline Road
Suite 101
Mesa, AZ 85206
tel: 001 480 882 0104
www.beadbox.com

Westcroft Beadworks, Inc.
149 Water Street
Norwalk CT 06854
tel: 001 800 2323761
www.beadworks.com

Buttons, Bangles and Beads
415 Corey Avenue
St Pete Beach FL 33706
tel: 001 727 363 4332
www.buttonsbanglesandbeads.com

Klews Expressions
104 West Panamint Avenue
Ridgecrest CA 93555
tel: 001 760 384 2323
www.klewexpressions.com

Shipwreck Beads
8560 Commerce Place Drive
NE Lacey WA 98516
tel: 001 360 754 2323
www.shipwreckbeads.com

WildAboutBeads.com
436 Main Road
Tiverton RI 02878-1314
tel: 001 401 624 4332
www.wildaboutbeads.com